I'm A Little Alien!

poems for LITTLE st★rs

Poems by
James Carter

Illustrations by
Mique Moriuchi

F
FRANCES LINCOLN
CHILDREN'S BOOKS

Contents

What a Lot of Poems!

Big poems,
little poems,
ones to make you
giggle poems.

Quiet poems,
LOUD poems,
weird 'n wild
'n WOW poems.

Paper, pen
and ink poems,
ones to make you
think poems.

Cheeky little
    chappy poems,
ones to make you
    happy poems.

Poems short
    poems l o n g.
You like poems?
    Let's read on …

I LIKE POEMS!

7

Let's Go!

Hello, world!
I've grown, you know.

I'm ready now.
It's time to go.

To build a boat
and sail away.

To ride a dragon
for a day.

To have a race
out into space.

Adventures are
the thing for me –

as long as I am
home for tea!

Space Poem

The sun is like
a gold balloon

the moon
a silver pearl

the earth is like
a marble blue

the milky way
a creamy swirl.

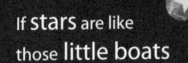

If **stars** are like
those **little boats**

afloat a **sea**
of **night**

the **dark** is when
a **hand** comes down

and switches
off **the light!**

Oggy!

Oggy was a robot.
He had planned to go
travelling to Jupiter
in his U-F-O.

He packed his this.
He packed his that.
His blue guitar.
His purple cat.

It took a while
to pack it all –
his map, his hat,
his bat and ball,

his bed, his boat,
his book, his broom.
His kitchen sink?
There wasn't room.

He locked the door.
He hummed awhile.
His radars bleeped.
He smiled a smile.

He pushed the button.
Time to go!
Engine started,
revved and ohhh…

It spluttered, made
a dreadful sound.
It lifted up then
crashed right down.

What was wrong?
His U-F-O
when stuffed with stuff
it would not go.

Oggy sighed.
He scratched his head.
He'd had enough.
And so, instead

he put his stuff
back in his shed.
And in a huff
he went to bed!

How To Speak Fluent Robot!

/\
Bleep.
Bleeep.
<(Bleeeeep.)>
Bleep!
!!!
!!
!!!!!
! Bleepy-bleep.!
!! Bleeeeeepy? !!
!! Bllllllllllleeep! !!
!! Bl-bl-bleep? !!
!! Bbbbbleep? !!
$ Bleepppp? #
B L E E P?
?? ??
?? ??
?? ??
?? ??
?? ??
?? ??
<BLEE EEEP!>

When I grow up I w**A**nt to be

crui**S**ing through the galaxy.

In my capsule, **T**here I'll be

passing through a sta**R**ry sea.

Captain **O**f my destiny.

Free from a**N**y gravity.

Like **A** feather floating free.

When I grow **U**p, an ASTRONAUT

is what I want **T**o be

!

How To Draw An Alien!

Do a
blobby body.

A face with
snakey tongues.

Three
gazey eyes
on sticky stalks.

Two curvy arms.
Two legs so long.

And
in the **sky**
a **splash** of **stars.**

A **spinning**
planet too.

See?
You've drawn
an **alien** ...

well done,
you!

Five Little Aliens

(Try this as a finger rhyme. Hide a finger with every verse, and bring them all back together at the end!)

FIVE little aliens
out on tour –
one heads home,
so then there were FOUR…

FOUR little aliens
out at sea –
one dives deep,
so then there were THREE…

THREE little aliens,
round the zoo –
one gets lost,
so then there were TWO…

TWO little aliens
in the sun –
one feels hot,
so then there was **ONE** …

ONE little alien
needs his chums –
zips off quick,
so then there were **NONE** …

FIVE little aliens
meet on the moon,
soar into space.
Off they **ZOOOOOM!**

Zim Zam Zoom!

Brown rocket
green rocket
first I've ever seen rocket
best there's ever been rocket

ZIM ZAM ZOOM!

Rush rocket
roar rocket
zip about some more rocket
let me climb aboard rocket

ZIM ZAM ZOOM!

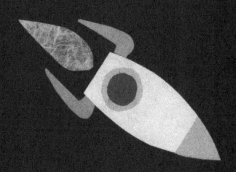

Blast rocket
fast rocket
overtaking Mars rocket
heading for the stars rocket

ZIM ZAM ZOOM!

Red rocket
blue rocket
racing to the moon rocket
won't you come back soon rocket

ZIM ZAM ZOOM!

It's Only Me!

Your night light.
Your silver sun.
Your ever bright
and cheery chum.

Who charms the stars,
the dark, the gloom?
Only me, your mate,
THE MOON!

One Little ALIEN!

```
        @     @
       ?     ?
       ?     ?
       I'm
    a little alien,
   cute and green,
    the grooviest
     guy you've
        never
        seen!
     !  Speedy like  !
    !!  a meteor, sparky  !!
   !!  like a star, spooky like  !!
  !!   a moonbeam, gleaming   !!
  !!    from afar. I whizz round   !!
  !!     Jupiter, Saturn and     !!
   !!       the sun. Yeah,      !!
      ?       I'm a little     ?
          alien, life
           is fun!
           !!    !!
           !!     !!
          !!       !!
          !!       !!
          !!       !!
        ????     ????
```

25

Saturn!

I love the stars
the moon the sun

but Saturn you're

my number *1*

Your rings are pearls
from deep blue seas
baubles hung
from Christmas trees
crystals in a
gloomy cavern
candles in a
hoop of heaven

With your fancy
silver rings
Saturn, you're
the King . . .
of
BLING!

(By James Carter, with Madeleine Carter)

27

Home Maker

Take a little planet
cushion it with cloud
pump it up with air and sky
start to spin around

Pour in plenty oceans
rivers, lakes and streams
liven up with animals
birds and human beings

Heat it in the middle
cool with gentle breeze
freeze it in the polar caps
lay down grass and trees

Let it dance around the sun
now it's fully grown
decorate with moon and stars
time to call it ... home!

Sweet Dreams

Once again
the **milky** moon
comes out
with **sugar** stars

For **honey** sun
has gone away
to visit
planet Mars

And all the world
is dreaming now
so sweetly
and so fine

Till honey sun
is back again
to bring us
breakfast time ...

Invitation to the Beach

Bring your bucket
bring your spade
bring your arm bands
bring your shades

Bring your frisbee
bring your hat
bring your flip flops
ball and bat

When you're ready
packed and done
don't forget
to bring the sun!

Bucket

Bucket full of seashells
bucket full of sea
bucket full of creatures
1-2-3!

Bucket full of seaweed
bucket full of sun
bucket full of memories
bucket full of fun!

Bucket full of holiday
bucket full of sand
bucket full of happiness
in my hand!

How To Build Your Very Own
Myrtle the Mermaid

Make
? with heaps ?
?? of golden ??
?? sand - her ??
??? tail, her ???
??? head ???
her
arms, her
!! hands. Gather !!
!! seaweed for her !!
!! hair - to shimmer !!
!! in the summer air. !!
!! Search for seashells !!
!! far and wide, use !!
!!! these for her !!!
smile, her
eyes.
Later,
when she's
all alone, tide will
come to take her home!

Little **by** Little **Fish**

Little by little
the little fish grew,
little by little
as little fish do.

A flipper, a fin,
a flapper or two,
skin all shimmery,
shiny and blue.

And moodier, yes,
and toothier too,
as many more gnashers
appeared anew.

Way down in the dark
that little fish grew

into a *SHARK!*

As little fish do.

Where Do You Sleep?

Where do you sleep, little dove?
In Mama's wing in the trees above.

Where do you sleep, little frog?
Next to the pond, on a big old log.

Where do you sleep, little bat?
Hung from the roof. It's nice like that!

Where do you sleep, little mouse?
Under the floorboards of this house!

Where do you sleep, little bug?
Here in the mud, where it's cool and snug!

Where do you sleep, little mole?
Oh, way, way down in a deep dark hole!

Where do you sleep, little bear?
In a winter cave. It's cosy there!

Where do you sleep, little you?
In bed with a ted and a blankie too!

The Terrible Ten!

One!

Do a stroll like a **tiger**

Two!

Do a grrr like a **bear**

Three!

Do a scuttle like a **spider**

Four!

Do a leap like a **hare**

Five!

Do a stretch like a **lion**

Six!

Do a flap like a **bat**

Seven!

Do a swoop like a **barn owl**

Eight!

Do a nibble like a **rat**

Nine!

Do a sway like an **eagle**

Ten!

Do a waddle like a **hen**

It might be nice
just once or twice
to do the ten … again!

Bew**AR**e!

There's a …

Jaw-snapper
teeth-gnasher
river-swimmer
dives-for-dinner

Fish-catcher
back-scratcher
cave-seeker
winter-sleeper

Forest-dweller
grizzly-fella

sneaking, lurking
here and there

you beware –

it's a **BEAR!**

You're . . .

. . . tall.
You're cute.
You're elegant.

More lovely
than an
elephant.

With purple
tongue
you dine
on leaves –

with head
held high
in towering
trees.

But you're
no freak,
you're just . . .
unique!

And big?
Not half!
You're a . . .

GIRAFFE!

f**ANT**astic

There's nothing wrong
with being small

so titchy that
the grass seems tall

more weeny than
a tiny twig

so little that
a mouse seems big!

That's how it is.
And we don't mind

for we are strong
as humankind!

How can we move

a gi**ANT** stick?

That's because we're

f**ANT**astic!

Conversation with a Fly

ZZZZ!

Oh, hello, fly!

ZZZZ!

What are you up to, then?

ZZZZ!

Sorry, I didn't catch that!

ZZZZ!

No, I still didn't get it!

ZZZZ!

Are you trying to tell me something?

ZZZZ!

Something important, perhaps?

ZZZZ!

Is something the matter maybe?

ZZZZ!

Are you in some kind of trouble?

ZZZZ!

Look. I don't understand 'zzzz!'

ZZZZ!

Please don't keep saying 'zzzz!'

ZZZZ!

Right, fly. I'll give you one more chance. Okay?

ZZZZZZZ!!!!

Odd Bod

A twitchy old thing
with two sad eyes

and a pointy snout
and a coat of spikes.

He's friendly? No!
He scuffles off.

He hides in a ball.
He looks in a huff.

He loves the night,
the dark, the fog.

What an odd
little bod
is a ... **hedgehog!**

Pond Poem

Once I was
a little dot.
Now I wriggle
such a lot.

Soon I'll have
a song and sing it,
then you'll hear my
ribbit ribbit!

Can you guess?
I bet you can –
I'm a ... **tadpole**
yes I am!

Mole and Elephant

"You can never have too many hills!"
said Mole, creating several more.
"Oh yes, you can!" said Elephant
and squished them into the floor.

"Okay, so what about holes?" said Mole,
and dug one deep as a well.
"Huh!" sneered Elephant, "call that a hole?"
And trumpeting,

d
  o
    w
    n

        h
       e

     f
      e
       l
        l

     !
     !

Conker Poem

Me, I'm a conker,
ripe and round.
I grow in a tree
then I drop to the ground.

My coat is green,
but I'm shiny-brown.
Me, I'm the best-dressed
seed around!

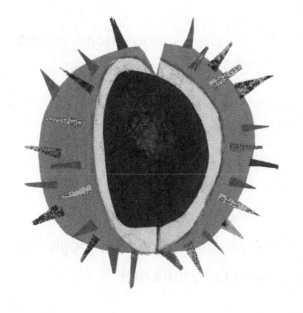

Egg!

It's like a snuggly home in here.
The wall is made of shell.
Am I eagle, puffin, owl?
Well, only time will tell.

Get ready for a crack to come.
And very soon you'll see —
bursting from this snuggly egg
is fluffy little me!

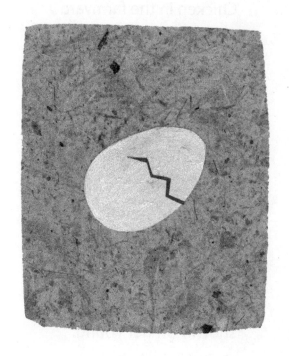

Chicken!

Chicken in the farmyard
cluckin' in the heat
strollin' and a struttin'
and a stretchin' her feet.

Chicken in the big barn
flappin' in the hay
wigglin' and a wrigglin'
and a layin' all day.

Chicken in the farmyard
showin' off her young:
six little chickadees
cheepin' in the sun!

Duck!

Hey, duck …
come back!

I want to hear
you quack!

I want to watch
your beak go snap!

Your two flat feet
go flippity-flap!

You've gone …

COME BACK!

Puffins!

They're such
multi-coloured things:
with **rainbow** beaks
and two **black** wings
and **orange** feet
and tummies **white**
plus **silver fish** –
for tea
each night!

Snowflake Song

I am a snowflake,
one of a billion,
built by cloud
to blanket ground.

Night falls. I fall,
downward spirals,
resting, settling,
journey done.

I am a snowflake,
silent, brilliant,
brief little angel,
going, gone.

Sky Poem

How high you are,
how w i d e you are,
how very **wet** then *dry* you are!

How blue you are,
how grey you are,
how stormy all the day you are!

Your clouds make puddles
on the ground.

Your light makes rainbows
bright and round.

Your sun makes seedlings
grow so fast.

Your night makes darkness,
moon and stars.

Whichever weather
you may do –
forever we'll look
up to you!

Ball P em

There's too
much *boing*
inside that ball.

I went
to bounce it
off the wall,

but then
it shot up
very high.

Now it's
stuck up in
the sky!

Funny Faces

Can you do a **big smile?**
Can you do a **wink?**
Can you do a **little nod?**
Can you do a **blink?**

Can you **shut** your **left eye?**
Can you **shut** your **right?**
Can you **wiggle** both your **ears?**
Can you **take** a **bite?**

Can you **wrinkle** up your **nose?**
Can you **lick** your **chin?**
Can you **puff** your **cheeks** up?
Can you do a **grin?**

Can you **raise** your **eyebrows?**
Can you **shake** your **hair?**
Can you **make** a **whistle?**
Can you do a **stare?**

Can you **pull** a **funny face?**
Can you **roll** your **tongue?**
Can you do these one more time?
Faces are **fun!**

Join the Band!

(Pretend to play as you go …)

If you want
to join **the band**
all you need
are your **two hands** . . .

Blow a **trumpet**
beat a **drum**
grab an **air guitar**
and strum.

You could bow
a **violin,**
why not have
a go and **sing?**

Pluck a **banjo**
toot a **flute**
honk a **sax**
and have a hoot!

Plink upon
a **ukulele**
faster, faster
going crazy!

Click your **fingers**
clap your **hands**
if you want
to join **the band!**

Shoes

Left shoe   right shoe!

Tell me where you're going to!

Will you walk along the hall,
down the stairs and out the door?

Will you skip along the street?
Will you tap out every beat?

Will you jump into a hole?
Will you score a winning goal?

Will you dance? Will you hop?
Will you shuffle, spin and stop?

Tell me now and tell me do …

Left shoe   right shoe!

Penny Pocket Poem

I found a tiny penny.

All shiny bright, like gold.

I popped it in my pocket here.

The one that has a ho

        o

         o

         o

         o

          o

         o

        o

       o

      o

     o

      o

       o

       o

         ole!

Whoops!

I had it in my **pocket**.
I had it in my **bag**.
I had it on my way to **school**.
I had it in my **hand**.

I had it in the **playground**.
I had it in the **hall**.
I had it just a while ago.
It's nowhere now at all.

I had it when I stroked the **cat**,
then when I went to **bed**.
Oh whoops!
It's here –
my favourite hat ...
It's right here
on my **HEAD**!

Fizz

How
much
fizz
will
fit
into a
bottle?
Well, at a
guess, I'd
say quite
a lot'll!

She's . . .

a *zing* of yellow,
the fizz in lemonade,
she's the path that keeps me safe,
my shelter and my shade.

She's Springtime's hope.
She's Autumn's gold.
She's Summer's coat
through Winter's cold.

My evening star,
my morning sun.
she's my world and more –
my mum!

Chatterbox

Mum thinks
I'm a
chatterbox.

I do like
talking – lots
and lots.

And when
I've nothing
left to say …

I'll keep on
chatting
anyway!

Me and My Mates

I've got a friend,
her name is Ruth.
She loves to wiggle
her wobbly tooth.

I've got a pal,
his name is Sam.
His favourite food
is strawberry jam.

I've got a chum,
his name is Tim.
He loves to play
the violin.

And last of all,
my sister Kate.
She's my mate.
And she's just great!

(Why not invent some of your own rhymes!)

Goodbye Rhyme

We're ready now
it's time to say
we've tidied up
we've cleared away

We've done our work
been out to play
we've learnt a lot
in just a day

We read a book
we talked, we sang
and in PE
we hopped, we ran

We looked for bugs
we caught a few
we watched them crawl
we drew them too

We're in our coats
and here we've sat
we're all together
on the mat

So now we've said
our goodbye rhyme
we'll all stand up …
it's homeward time!

Hello and Goodbye

An H, an E, a double L,
a curly-wurly O –
you put them all together
and they say HELLO!

A **G** and then a double **O**,
a **D**, a **B**, a **Y**.
And finally … it's just an **E**,
and time to say **GOODBYE!**

Sleepy?

I'm not sleepy,
I'm not tired,
I'm not going to bed –
beneath the stars
above the stairs,
I'm chatting
with my ted.

What's that, Ted?
You're snoozy, yes?
I'll tell you
what I'll do –
I'll come and keep
you warm in bed
and teddysit
for you!

What's . . .

. . . Christmassy-cosy?
What's snug as an egg?
What warms up your toesies?
What cushions your head?

That loveliest, comfiest place that is . . .

BED!

Dream Train

At Yawnington Station
down Lullaby Lane
in Bedfordshire County
we all board the train

Past Cosytown Towers
and Dreamyville Park
the little lights shining
it's late and it's dark

Past Winter Bear Mountain
and Sleepy Dust Moon
the train is now braking
as ever so soon

You will be waking
it's morning again
at Yawnington Station
down Lullaby Lane

JAMES CARTER is an award-winning children's poet and educational writer. He travels all over the UK and abroad (with his guitar, Keith) to schools, libraries and festivals to give lively poetry and music performances as well as workshops, Creative Writing days and INSET sessions.

I'm A Little Alien! is a companion collection to his other Frances Lincoln title, *Hey, Little Bug!* James lives in Oxfordshire with his one wife, two daughters, three acoustic guitars and four or so billion books.

www.jamescarterpoet.co.uk

MORE POETRY FROM
FRANCES LINCOLN CHILDREN'S BOOKS

978-1-84780-367-2

A brilliant, varied collection of poems for very young
children, suitable for early years and Key Stage One.
Funny, sad, silly, sing-along, the poems are about friends
and families, pets and creatures, school, space travel
and more. There is something for everyone in this
sparkling collection – with lots of action and joining in.

'Delightful and kind humour bubbles through this
collection … A perfect introduction to poetry for the
youngest readers.' – *LoveReading4Kids*

978-1-84780-168-5

Perfect for Early Years and Infant classrooms, and for older children too, these poems are fresh, funny and brilliant for reading aloud.

'What shines through is a real understanding of the target audience and the things that will appeal to them. A great book for the classroom/school library.'
– *Bookseller*